Written by Anne Singh
Illustrated by Aline Riquier

Specialist Adviser:
Raghubir Singh

ISBN 0-944589-14-6
First U.S. Publication 1988 by
Young Discovery Library
217 Main St. • Ossining, NY 10562

©1985 by Editions Gallimard
Translated by Sarah Matthews
English text © 1987 by Moonlight Publishing Ltd.
Thanks to Aileen Buhl

YOUNG DISCOVERY LIBRARY

Living in India

Imagine you are in a busy city street…

YOUNG DISCOVERY LIBRARY

eople on foot thread their way in
etween buffalo carts, cars, trucks and
ckshaws. Horns sound, people shout,
oats, cows and even elephants walk the
reets. Monkeys leap from rooftop to
ooftop and sneak down to steal fruit
and vegetables
from the little
shops.

kshaw, a three-wheeled taxi

**his is India, with six hundred and
ighty-five million inhabitants:** it is
ne most populated country in the
orld after China. It is separated from
hina by the
imalayas, the highest
ountains in
ne world. India is
uge, and there are all sorts
 different
nds of country: deserts,
ains, jungles…Most
idians live in the
ountryside. But the
wns are very full too.

Naga warrior of Mongol descent. The Nagas live at the foothills of the Himalayas.

Peasant from Rajasthan. Three-thousand years ago his ancestors arrived in India from Central Asia

Farmer from Kerala of Dravidian descent. His ancestors were driven down into the south.

Negrito from the Andaman Islands in the Indian Ocean

The damp jungles of the Bengal delta are home to cobras, deer, rhinoceros, storks, crocodiles, monkeys and tigers.

In Rajasthan, there are camels, antelopes and elephants. In Gujerat there are even a few lions...

In the south, along the edges of the rice fields, there are elephants, herons, macaws and wild buffaloes.

The capital of India is New Delhi. India is one-third the size of the United States, but has more than three times as many people.

HIMALAYAS
NEW DELHI
GANGES
RAJASTHAN   VARANASI
CALCUTTA
BAY
OF
BOMBAY   BENGAL
MADRAS
KERALA   ANDAMAN
ISLANDS

9

The wind is beginning to blow. Clouds are scudding across the sky. Then rain starts to fall, more and more of it, and storms flash and rumble. **This is the monsoon,** when the rains come and water soaks into the earth which has been baked dry by months of sunshine. Although many fields now have irrigation, the monsoon is still very important. Without it the farmers would have hardly anything to harvest and they would go hungry. But if the monsoon is too violent, then the crops are damaged, and that means not enough to eat as well. After the monsoon has passed, winter sets in. In the north, the nights are cold, and people wrap up well to keep warm. In the south, winter is mild. Summer starts around the end of March. By May it is so hot that the tar melts on the roadways. In the houses, big fans make a cooling breeze. At night, people sleep out of doors.

During the monsoon there are often floods

villages in the north, young girls celebrate the coming of
e rains.

ings grow thick and green in the south where the monsoon
ls heavily. The rice fields are watered by little canals.

the Thar desert, in Rajasthan, women come to fetch water
om a slowly drying pool.

Buffaloes hauling water from the river to water the fields

Farming is hard work!

Men, women and children all help in the fields together. They have buffaloes and camels to pull their carts and more and more tractors too. Canals and electric pumps carry water to the rice fields, and to the fields of wheat and millet. As the fields get bigger the wildlife is being pushed back. Most tigers and panthers now live protected in wildlife reserves.

India is the world's foremost producer of tea. The Indians of South India drink tea all day long. Shopkeepers will offer you a cup while you're out shopping…

Tea plants grow in the hills in the northeast and the south of the country.

Peasants often paint the horns of the cows and buffaloes

Would you like to go to school by boat?

A lot of children in Kerala do. Kerala is a region of rice fields and spice plantations. The sea weaves its inlets in and out of the land. The people travel by boat along the lagoons and canals. You can see families of elephants bathing in the lakes and rivers. There are a lot of fishermen here. The pepper that your mother uses in her cooking may have come from Kerala. Merchants have traded in Kerala pepper for hundreds of years.

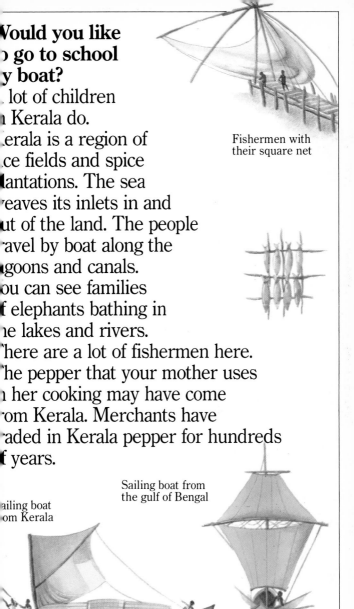

Fishermen with their square net

Sailing boat from Kerala

Sailing boat from the gulf of Bengal

Grain is kept in raised storehouses.

A woman plasters the walls of her house with mud.

In this village in Rajasthan,

the walls of the houses are a mixture of mud and straw. The roofs are made of thatch. The peasants sleep on string beds and keep their things

Cow dung drying in the sun

in painted tin trunks. The women dry cow dung cakes to use as fuel for their cooking fires. There is a tree called the **neem.** It is an important tree in the village. Statues of the local gods are kept underneath it. The peasants leave offerings of rice and flowers, and light little oil lamps to ensure the gods' protection. They clean their teeth with twigs from the neem tree because of its medicinal qualities. There is even a neem toothpaste for townspeople.

Making chapatis

How do Indians eat?

With the fingers of the right hand. Meals are usually accompanied by a dish of rice, or by cakes of wheat or millet called **chapatis,** which are used to pick up the meat or vegetables. There are many different **curries,** delicious, highly-spiced stews made of meat or fish or vegetables.

Puddings are very sweet, and made from saffron, rose water or coconut. Tea is often flavored with cinnamon, cardamom and cloves.

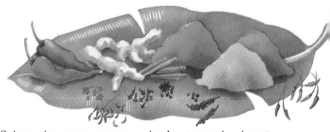

Spices: cinnamon, pepper, coriander, turmeric, pimento, cloves, cardamom, ginger, cumin, aniseed, saffron, all laid on a banana leaf

Coconut, mango, banana, papaya

Did you know that Hindus will never kill a cow?

In olden days, they were afraid of running out of milk. Now the cow is a sacred animal. Some Indians regard all living things as sacred. They are vegetarians, and will never eat meat or fish or eggs. Others will only eat meat on family feast days.

Dishes are placed around the rice on a big metal platter called a thali.

What sort of clothes do Indians wear?

Women wear a **sari.** This is a brightly-colored piece of silk or cotton cloth which is several yards long, wrapped  around the waist and then draped over the left shoulder. In western India, peasant women wear a full skirt, a little blouse decorated with mirror spangles, and a long veil. The men wear a **kurta**, a collarless shirt, over **churidar**, tight cotton trousers, or over a **dhoti**, a length of cloth wrapped around the waist and tucked between the legs.

If a woman wears red powder worked
into the parting of her hair, it means she
is married.
Women also decorate their foreheads
with a dot of red paint, a **tika.**

They wear wonderful jewels.
In the country, they are
heavy and made of silver;
in the towns, they are
fine and made of gold.
Often they are set
with precious stones.
These jewels
represent most of
the family riches,
and the peasant
women wear them
day and night.

Jewels worn
by women in
Rajasthan

In the towns, the men wear European
clothes.

The bridegroom arriv
at his fiancée's hous
on a beautifully dresse
horse, accompanied l
a young brother or cousi

Often, parents choose husbands and wives for their children.

Indians very rarely marry outside their own social and religious group, or **caste.** An astrologer makes sure that the bride's and bridegroom's horoscopes are well-matched. Then he decides the best date for the wedding. In Rajasthan, the ceremony takes place at night at the bride's house. The bride and groom, dressed in the finest silk and brocade, walk seven times around a holy fire. The groom lifts up the bride's veil; this may be the first time he has seen her. Weddings are magnificent and cost a lot of money. The couple live in the groom's house, where the groom's mother rules the household.

The bride's hands and feet are decorated with fine patterns traced in a vegetable dye called henna.

Ganesh   Kali   Buddha   Hanuman

The majority of Indians belong to the
Hindu religion.
**For the Hindus, God has thirty-
three million different forms.**
The three main forms are Brahma,
Vishnu and Shiva. Children learn
about them by hearing stories
from the Ramayana and the
Mahabharata, long
tales all about the
gods and their
battles.

A Brahman priest

Families go together to the temples
and lay wreaths of flowers at the gods' feet.

Muslims pray to Allah, their name for God, by kneeling and bowing down five times a day.

Sikhs wear daggers in their turbans.

ne Hindus believe that
ter somebody has died
e soul is born again
some other living thing:
person, animal or insect.
his is called **reincarnation.**
here are seventy-five million
uslims in India, and
er sixteen million Christians.
is one of the oldest
hristian communities
the world. Buddhism
gan in India, and
s spread from there
roughout Asia.

rims kiss the feet of
atue of Bahubali, a Jain god.

The Jains respect all life, even that of insects.

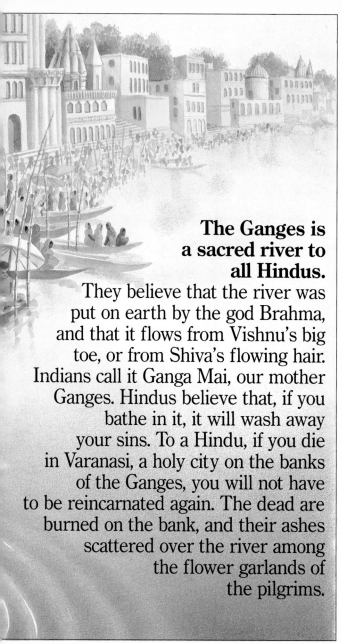

The Ganges is a sacred river to all Hindus.
They believe that the river was put on earth by the god Brahma, and that it flows from Vishnu's big toe, or from Shiva's flowing hair. Indians call it Ganga Mai, our mother Ganges. Hindus believe that, if you bathe in it, it will wash away your sins. To a Hindu, if you die in Varanasi, a holy city on the banks of the Ganges, you will not have to be reincarnated again. The dead are burned on the bank, and their ashes scattered over the river among the flower garlands of the pilgrims.

The festival of Holi
is celebrated with
flags and drums

**India is a land
of festivals!**
There are feasts
to celebrate all the
thousands of gods.
Some feasts last for
several days. **Diwali is
the Festival of Light.** In the northern
part of the country they celebrate
Diwali at the new year. Each house
glimmers with hundreds of tiny oil
lamps, and children set off fireworks.
Holi is a spring harvest festival.
People dance through the streets,
scattering water and red powder.
Dassehra is a festival celebrating the
victory of Rama, the hero god of the
Ramayana stories, over Ravana, a
ten-headed demon. Ravana
kidnapped Sita, Rama's wife, but
Hanuman the monkey god and all
his monkey tribe rescued her.

In Bombay, the festival of Ganpati is held in honor of Ganesh, the elephant god.

In Calcutta, there is a festival for Kali, a goddess with ten arms.

In Kerala, during the festival of Trichur Pooram, people compete to have the most beautiful umbrellas.

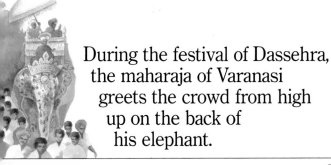

During the festival of Dassehra, the maharaja of Varanasi greets the crowd from high up on the back of his elephant.

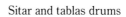

Sitar and tablas drums

Music and dance are an important part of daily life.

Did you know that Indian musicians don't read the music that they play? They make it up as they go along. There are special kinds of tunes to play in the afternoon, in the evening and at night. Musicians play the sitar or the tambura, accompanied by the little tablas drums, played with the fingertips. There are all kinds of music. Often in the countryside you can hear a flute singing clearly in the night air.

Kathakali actors with their painted faces

Indian dancers

you go walking in the streets, you may meet dancing
ars, trained monkeys, snake charmers, acrobats...

dian dancers can speak with
heir hands. They use their
ands and their eyes to tell stories
d to conjure up feelings: sadness,
ve, fear. They can mime a woman
rawing water from a well, a river
owing, nectar dripping...

takes more than four hours to
ake up an actor for Kathakali, the
aditional theater of the Kerala region.
ometimes the actors fall asleep while
ey are being made up, in order to rest
r the evening ahead!

kirs may stretch out
spiny cactus leaves,
bury themselves
to the neck
sand, to do
nance for their sins.
ssersby give them donations.

In the villages, school is often held out of doors, with the blackboard propped up against a tree.

There are fifteen main languages, and fourteen ways of writing.
The national language is Hindi, but a lot of people speak English too. And there are five hundred different dialects as well.

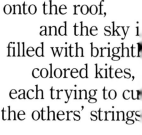

Children play with hoops.

Do you like playing with a kite?
A lot of Indian children do. In January there is a big kite festival. The whole family climbs up onto the roof, and the sky is filled with brightly colored kites, each trying to cut the others' strings.

The Indians love to play cricket.

Which country in the world makes the most films? India! **They make at least eight-hundred films a year.** The Indians love going to the movies. All the family, even the babies, go together.

India is a country full of a mixture of old and new — alongside buffaloes tilling the fields stand satellite tracking stations. Its history has been shaped by all sorts of different peoples and different traditions. For a long time, India was ruled by the Moguls. Then it was ruled by the English. Since 1947 it has been independent.

In The Bazaars of Hyderabad

by Sarojini Naidu

What do you sell, O ye merchants?
Richly your wares are displayed.
Turbans of crimson and silver,
Tunics of purple brocade,
Mirrors with panels of amber,
Daggers with handles of jade.

What do you weigh, O ye vendors?
Saffron and lentil and rice.
What do you grind, O ye maidens?
Sandlewood, henna and spice.
What do you call, O ye peddlers?
Chessmen and ivory dice.

What do you make, O ye goldsmith
Wrislet and anklet and ring,
Bells for the feet of blue pigeons,
Frail as a dragonfly's wing,
Girdles of gold for the dancers,
Scabbards of gold for the king.

What do you cry, O ye fruitmen?
Citron, pomegranate and plum.
What do you play, O musicians?
Sitar, tambura and drum.
What do you chant, O magicians?
Spells for the ages to come.

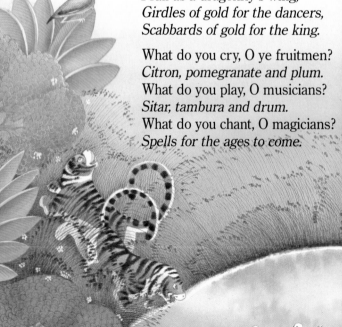